MARGARET CALKIN JAMES

AT THE SIGN OF THE RAINBOW

MARGARET CALKIN JAMES 1895 – 1985

Betty Miles

Published by Felix Scribo 1996

Betty Miles trained as a painter/printmaker at Birmingham College of Art, and practised for some years as an artist and illustrator. As a postgraduate student in the History of Art and Design at Brighton and Sussex Universities she contributed to the exhibition and publication *Women Designers Between the Wars* in 1993. Her article on CH and MC James is published in the *Journal of the Decorative Arts Society*, no. 20, 1996.

Alan Powers is a freelance critic and art historian based in London.

Text © Betty Miles 1996

Published 1996 by Felix Scribo
2 Arrow Grange, nr. Alcester, Warwickshire B49 5PJ
01789-764272

A CIP catalogue record of this book is available from the British Library

ISBN 0 9528481 0 4

Colour photographs by Prudence Cuming Associates Limited, London W1 except where credited London Transport Museum
Colour reproduction by System Colour Limited, London SW6
Printed by G&B Colour Printers, Teddington
Designed and typeset by Philip Miles, Brighton

Front and back cover: detail from the signboard for the Rainbow Workshops, Great Russell Street, 1920. Painted wood.
Title page: Margaret Calkin working at her calligraphy table, 1915.

ACKNOWLEDGEMENTS

A great debt of gratitude is due to Betty and Philip Miles whose devotion to this project has touched and inspired me. Their enthusiasm for Margaret's work has made me look at it with fresh eyes and Betty's meticulous research has uncovered facets of my parents' life of which I had no conception. I am also very grateful to Alan Powers for his helpful advice and encouragement, and particularly for writing the Foreword.

It was David Ellis of the London Transport Museum who first urged me to write a book. Undaunted by my point-blank refusal he has given the most generous and practical support in offering access to the Museum's archive transparencies and giving permission to reproduce their copyright material.

Without the immediate and generous response of my first sponsor, Lloyd's of London, the whole project would undoubtedly have fallen by the wayside, so formidable was the list of refusals that followed. However, others have agreed to help in various ways, in lending material or in further financial support, and they are included in the list of names overleaf. I wish especially to thank two of my cousins, Ann Lord and Robert Calkin, for their belief in me and for their encouragement 'in the cloudy and dark day', as well as for their very generous financial support.

We would like to put on record the fact that if Hedley Picton, then head of the Art Department at the London Central YMCA, had not accepted an exhibition of Margaret Calkin James's work in 1982 and had not then written a charming article, 'Rainbow Lady', it is doubtful that Betty, Philip and I would ever have met. A fact that gives cause for gratitude.

Finally, an inestimable thank you to my mother, Margaret Calkin James, who through her character and life's work gave such enduring pleasure to so many people, especially me. This undertaking has been the greatest pleasure and privilege of my life and I hope that we have maintained the standards set by my remarkable mother whose total dedication to the work in hand never intruded on the love, joy, care and patience afforded her family.

Elizabeth Argent

With thanks to:

Her Majesty The Queen

Jeremy and Christine Bradshaw

Ian B Calkin
Robert Riviere Calkin

Robin Calkin
Val J Calkin

Calkin, Pattinson & Co Ltd

CT Delaney

Lloyd's of London

London Regional Transport

London Transport Museum – David Ellis

Ann S Lord

System Colour Limited

The Worshipful Company of Scriveners

FOREWORD

More than twenty years ago, in the springtime of the Art Deco revival, one could buy examples of the real thing, surviving in the form of Curwen Press Pattern Papers, from the Curwen Gallery in Colville Place. These were designs by luminaries like Paul Nash and Edward Bawden, commissioned in the 1920s by Oliver Simon to provide a machine-made alternative to the then-fashionable hand-blocked papers from Italy. Among the papers, one of the most attractive and jazzy was a three-colour chevron which I pasted onto the boards of a notebook. In 1987, when I organised an exhibition at Judd Street Gallery to launch the Whittington Press book on Curwen Papers, I found the name of Margaret James as the author of this design, one of the first and most successful in the Curwen range. It was only in 1994, on seeing the *Women Designing: Redefining Design in Britain between the Wars* exhibition and reading Betty Miles's catalogue essay on Margaret Calkin James that it all fell into place, for although I knew something of CH James, the architect of Wells House flats in Hampstead and many fine public buildings, history had until then overlooked his wife, perhaps the more talented of the two. The contrast reveals how in architecture the Arts and Crafts movement became conservative and classical in the 1920s, while the decorative arts, particularly the work of women, somehow retained boldness with delicacy.

Photograph of Margaret Calkin in 1917.

Margaret Calkin James's designs were the most lively in *Women Designing*. She belonged to her period, as her bobbed-hair photograph suggests, but her work is still fresh, like that of her contemporaries, Susie Cooper and Enid Marx. The influence of the pre-1914 London avant-garde persists in her strong colours and delight in geometry. She also carried on the ideals of the Omega Workshops in her own Rainbow Workshops by making design into an adventure in which small things mattered as much as large and creativity was synonymous with enjoyment. Her firm principles as a Christian Scientist kept her going through her later life, when she was disabled by a stroke, yet went on designing embroideries.

It is a great benefit of feminism in art and design history that work by such artists, although not great in quantity, should be rediscovered and appraised. It has a quality that stands on its own, as Margaret James's pattern papers do in company with designs by some of her greatest contemporaries.

Alan Powers

8

Margaret Calkin James, 1935.
When working in her studio she always wore a blue cotton smock, replaced when necessary from a French paper pattern.
The clothes she made for herself and subsequently for her children were plain, stylish and uncluttered, in keeping with her 'simple life' ideals.

MARGARET CALKIN JAMES 1895 – 1985

In 1861 William Morris and associates established a business in Red Lion Square that promoted all aspects of architecture and the decorative arts. Such versatility was compared at the time with that of the Italian painters of the Middle Ages. Sixty years later the 'good work' of Miss Margaret B Calkin in her Rainbow Workshops was reviewed in *Colour* magazine (October 1921) and also likened to an early Italian painter's studio, with the rider that 'there is no attempt to imitate the past but, on the contrary, a keen attention to the requirements of modern life'. Her flexible, eclectic approach embodied Morris's Arts and Crafts ideal of the well-rounded designer – a glance at her order book shows that she was regularly employed in graphics, calligraphy, stage design, textile printing, watercolour painting and printmaking. She worked for the most progressive, prestigious and popular clients of the inter-war years. *Colour* magazine also reviewed – coincidentally on the same page – the 'daring experiments' being carried out by CH James, her future husband. His work was cited as evidence that at least some architects 'are building in the conviction that beauty is a consequence of purpose perfectly fulfilled'.

Harry Bernard Calkin married Margaret Agnes Palfrey in 1890, and Margaret Bernard, born in 1895, was the third of seven siblings, all of whom shared their father's middle name. Harry Calkin was in insurance and became a Lloyd's Underwriter in 1910. The family lived comfortably in Heath Drive, Hampstead. Reputed to be 'the straightest man in the city', Harry imparted to his children his own ideals of strict personal integrity and of service to others. In this he was ably assisted by his wife, who made sure that her daughters were well-versed in home economics and in patient application to hard work. Young Margaret's early introduction to practical household skills was an invaluable supplement to her creativity.

For a young lady of Miss Calkin's standing there was no financial necessity for a career; art, like music, was a desirable social accomplishment. Less conventional was her decision to become a professional artist. However, craftsmen and artists had featured in previous generations. Powell Penry Palfrey (1830 – 1902), her maternal grandfather, was a skilled draughtsman and noted painter of horses. Coaching scenes and Derby winners for the aristocracy and for Edward VII were his line, and he also produced heraldic designs and stained glass. On Margaret's father's side the bookbinding firm, Robert Riviere and Sons, founded by her great-grandfather, employed her favourite Uncle Arthur,

Portrait of Harry Bernard Calkin
(1861 – 1926) by Lance Calkin, his brother.
Reproduced with permission from
Calkin Pattison & Co Ltd.

Coaches in snow by Powell Penry Palfrey,
1880.

Harry's brother. So, although taken aback, the Calkin family was not unsympathetic to Margaret's vocation.

Calkin entered the Central School of Arts and Crafts in 1914. A woman of her social standing and abilities might have been expected to opt for a fine art training at a time when the crafts were not highly esteemed by institutions like the Royal Academy of Arts. She preferred to embark on a course that offered links with industry and more practical usefulness. She adopted a multi-disciplinary approach which helped to erode the hierarchical barriers between the fine and decorative arts. Her adaptability was later to prove necessary in the economic stringency of the Depression, but she also strove to challenge the art establishment and make the visual arts more relevant to public life. (In 1915 Wyndham Lewis accurately predicted that poster advertisements would educate public taste better than picture galleries.)

At the Central School Calkin learned to appreciate the outlook of its founder, WR Lethaby. Priority was given to acquiring skills and Calkin specialised in calligraphy, winning a Queen's Scholarship in 1915. She then progressed to larger-scale activities but never relinquished the painstaking precision of calligraphy. The Westminster School of Art in Vincent Square founded an innovatory class focused on design for advertising and retailing, including posters, three-dimensional construction of figures and sets and the use of lighting in shop windows. Most important was the weaving of these elements into a unified design. Calkin, who had a pronounced theatrical bent, quickly transferred these new concepts to stage, property and costume design – she appeared in the title role of *The Birth of a Pearl*, a tableau mounted by Westminster students for the Chelsea Arts Ball .

In 1916 the Arts and Crafts Exhibition Society staged their Eleventh Annual Exhibition. Calkin was one of the Westminster student volunteers who laboured by the side of the exhibition architect Frank Troup to transform the galleries at the Royal Academy of Arts. (Half a century later she recalled in a letter that Troup, nearly 60, grew so fond as to declare his intentions: 'He wrote to mother first who had to say no – I was 19! … he certainly was a dear!') The 1916 exhibition was well publicised amidst the privations of war and it is clear from press reports that calligraphy was in demand, perhaps increasingly so: 'Rolls of Honour, Litanies, Canticles and so forth, penned in black or wrought in gleaming gold by that master scriptist Mr Graily Hewitt, who has an apt pupil in Miss Margaret Calkin.' Here Calkin was publicly associated with an acknowledged master of the revival of calligraphy. Graily Hewitt, himself a former pupil of Edward Johnston, initiated her into the complexities of gilded illumination, always insisting that a sound technique was the prerequisite for free and confident self-expression.

The sentimentality and elevated moral feeling of the Arts and Crafts Exhibition of 1916 was described by Roger Fry as 'genteel nonsense'. Indeed it was forlorn to hope that economic problems might still be solved by the old Arts and Crafts solutions. By then WR Lethaby and other design reformers believed that Britain's declining industries needed improved design on an industrial scale and a marketplace of more educated and discerning consumers. In 1914 Lethaby helped to found the Design and Industries Association (DIA). 'Fitness for purpose' was the theoretical foundation of Calkin's practical training. Her own words, published in the October 1921 article in *Colour* magazine, bear out her early dedication to a functionalist credo: 'If we would all begin at home and be satisfied with bare necessities, banishing from our lives all those things that not only are not made or fitted for a specific purpose, but

Margaret Calkin James and her husband CH James on honeymoon, 1922. To family and friends they were affectionately known as Jane and Jimmy.

Ark and Rainbow, flanked on each side by the Deluge and Mount Ararat.
'Begin at home' said Margaret Calkin James, who installed this carved and painted wooden sign above the front door of 1 Hampstead Way, where she used the top floor as her workshop from 1922 to 1929.

that we could do without, we should then find that the country would only produce the things that mattered, that work would be done well, and the workers would be happy.'

During the war women discovered that they could do many 'men's jobs' perfectly well. One such job was Calkin's first post: as head of the Art Department of the Central London YMCA she was responsible for the selection of some sixty thousand pictures and for the design and execution of numerous decorative schemes, friezes and curtains for YMCA Red Triangle army huts overseas. Her prodigious efforts were hailed in *Queen* magazine as 'a labour of love'. The experience and confidence gained at the YMCA was invaluable to Calkin and when the Art Department was closed down she took over the premises as her own Rainbow Workshops, retaining the existing goodwill and steadily building up a wider reputation. Hers was one of a burgeoning movement of similar ventures that brought artists into direct contact with the public, bypassing a notoriously conservative network of wholesalers and retailers.

In 1921 the British Institute of Industrial Art, sponsored by the Boards of Education and Trade, mounted the British Industries Fair in which one of Calkin's 'Mayflower' banners was noted as an exemplar of 'the increasing share that women are taking', not only as buyers for great firms but also in the actual 'design of things that we buy to add to the pleasure of our domestic surroundings.' No visual record of this touring Mayflower Pageant survives but

RAINBOW

WORKSHOPS

Signboard for the Rainbow Workshops, 1920. Painted wood, double-sided, showing Margaret Calkin's chosen emblem – an ark of refuge with a rainbow of promise.
A photograph of this hanging sign appeared in the Signs and Tablets section of the DIA Yearbook of 1922. In the same year she married CH James, closed the Rainbow Workshops and went to live in the house he had designed at 1 Hampstead Way.
The Design and Industries Association listed their membership and subscriptions in 'Members Rules and Activities' as follows:
JAMES, Chas. Holloway, A.R.I.B.A., *Architect*, 15 Gower Street, W.C.1. [£1.1s.]
JAMES, Mrs. M. Calkin, 1 Hampstead Way, N.W.3 [10s. 6d.].

Ark and Rainbow symbol.
One of various permutations of this theme devised by Margaret Calkin James for letterheads and rubber stamps.

Matilda, who told lies and was burned to death. One of several illustrations by Margaret Calkin for the programme of *Four Cautionary Tales and a Moral* by Hilaire Belloc. (Belloc is now remembered chiefly for his light verse but in the early years of the century he was a popular satirist, polemicist and challenger of settled assumptions.)

Press cutting from the *Daily Graphic*, 7 January 1920, showing Margaret Calkin (right) as Matilda. This production was held in January 1920 at King George's Hall, London Central YMCA in aid of the YMCA National Appeal.

the style and spirit of these 'striking banners' had a preamble that was also much photographed and reported. This was Calkin's adaptation, as a series of vivid *tableaux vivants*, of Hilaire Belloc's *Cautionary Tales* at the YMCA. Her costumes, props and stage sets were in the very latest jazz-age style: 'Firemen in Futurist Costumes!' ran one of many enthusiastic press headlines, which went on to commend her 'excellent miming' in a variety of tragicomic roles. The *AA Journal* praised the 'brilliant conventionalism' of her backdrops, her Egyptienesque costumes, her 'fantastically ingenious and pleasing props, especially the orange lion with the emerald eyes' and finally her own 'spirited performance'. CB Cochrane, the famous promoter and producer of West End entertainments, was an enthusiastic supporter of young artists and of new

ALBERT HALL BALL REHEARSAL. Students at the Westminster School of Art, Vincent-square, rehearsing their tableau " The Birth of a Pearl " for the Chelsea Arts Ball next month.

methods of publicity. The success of his Revue *The League of Notions*, sending up the League that was optimistically expected to end all wars, was due in no small measure to Calkin's humorous and imaginative sets and publicity.

Marriage in 1922 meant the end of Calkin's independent endeavours at the Rainbow Workshops. Mrs Calkin James's primary role in the eyes of society

Press cutting from *The Daily Star*, 2 January, 1920. Margaret Calkin in the title role of *The Birth of a Pearl*.

Illuminated and gilded title pages for Lloyd's 'Address from the Brokers to the Underwriters', 1928. The sailing ship depicted is the Lutine of 1688 whose bell was still rung daily in the Lloyd's building. The stylised Arts and Crafts medievalism of the decorations and the old ship contrast boldly with those great symbols of modernity, the ocean liners of the Cunard and Orion lines. Stylised waves recall the water on the Rainbow Workshops sign. The two bands of 'flames' use a device that Calkin's Uncle Arthur, the bookbinder, had noticed on a stage backdrop for the fire scene in her 1920 production of Belloc's *Cautionary Tales*. These, he said, were a favourite ornament of the old bookbinding masters.

This loyal address was worked on vellum and bound by Robert Riviere, where Uncle Arthur worked.

Speedwell
Northwood
Middx.   July 1. 1915.

My Dear Miss Calkin,

Marjorie told me that she had heard from you that you have had private information of your success in The Queen's Scholarship Competition. I am aware that you did not wish me to be told until it was officially announced, but since I have known it from the very day of the judging! perhaps you will condone my impatience in offering you my best congratulations without further delay. I saw the show, & I consider that no sensible judges could have decided otherwise. It would be as useless, I know, as it would be ill-advised to tell you not to continue to be so modest about yourself, but I do hope you won't go on suggesting to yourself that there are certain things which you can't do. We hear a lot about 'The will to conquer' in these days: I'm sure this delightfully unexpected success — unexpected by you, that is, will help you to cultivate it! I would dare wager that I'm not the only one with plenty of faith in your ability.

sincerely yours
Karl Parsons.

Letter to Miss Calkin from Karl Parsons, who had been teaching stained glass at the Central School since 1904. He wrote to offer warmest congratulations when she was designated Queen's Scholar in 1915: her sample of calligraphy submitted to this scholarship competition came top. The honour, even more than the money, was much prized by family and by friends, to assure her that everyone had great faith in her ability and to suggest that she 'should not continue to be so modest' about herself. Doubtless this 'modesty' was part of her charm and of making her way as a woman in a sphere where women were vastly outnumbered.

FOREWORD

"The Adoration of the Soldiers" is a short mystery play which was suggested to Mons: Cammaerts during a visit which he paid to the Belgian Trenches in Christmas Week. It is written in the manner of the old mediaeval French and English Nativity Plays, and with the same genuine and almost childish simplicity. In introducing the Virgin and Child among modern soldiers in a miserable dug-out, the author has endeavoured to show that the spirit for which we are fighting today is fundamentally the same as that which prompted the Crusades and erected the Cathedrals in the Middle Ages.

The English translation is by Madame Tita Brand-Cammaerts and the script has been written by Margaret B. Calkin

The First World War formed a melancholy back-drop to Margaret's training. In 1916 *The Adoration of the Shepherds,* a Christmas Allegory specially written in tribute to soldiers in the Belgian trenches was published by the Fine Art Society with text in French and English penned by Margaret Calkin as a 'labour of love'. The architect Frank Troup, who was a founder member of staff at the Central School, wrote in praise of the script and assured Mrs Calkin that her daughter's mere involvement in such an honourable endeavour was 'sufficient reward in itself'.

Calkin was a founder member of the Society of Scribes and Illuminators, formed in 1921.

MAY IT PLEASE YOUR MAJESTY. A LITTLE MORE THAN A CENTURY AGO A QUEEN of this Realm, then in the early years of her reign, to the delight of her loyal subjects in the City of London, came to the City and opened the new Royal Exchange—a building that was the home of Lloyd's for nearly ninety years. Now another Queen of the Realm to our great happiness honours our Society with her presence, to lay the Foundation Stone of another building that will soon be added to our present home. While we proffer our humble duty to Your Majesty we pray that under God's Providence Your Majesty's reign may be as rich in blessings for mankind as was that of Your Majesty's great ancestress Queen Victoria. MAY we also remind Your Majesty that

Illuminated and gilded title pages for Lloyd's 'Address to Her Majesty the Queen', 1952. This and two other loyal addresses , to King George V (1928) and to Her Majesty Queen Elizabeth The Queen Mother (1957), were made in duplicate by Calkin James. Lloyd's was shrewd to be thus insured as the 1928 original was destroyed in the Buckingham Palace bombing of 1940.

MAY   IT PLEASE YOUR MAJESTY,
LITTLE MORE THAN A
CENTURY AGO A QUEEN
of this Realm, then in the
early years of her reign, to
the delight of her loyal subjects in the City of London,
came to the City and opened the new Royal
Exchange~a building that was the home of
Lloyd's for nearly ninety years. Now another
Queen of the Realm to our great happiness
honours our Society with her presence, to lay
the Foundation Stone of another building
that will soon be added to our present home.

was now the running of a home and the care of her war-wounded husband. By the end of the decade her duties included the rearing of three children, Brian, Alison and Elizabeth. Adapting to the new situation, her studios were to be private, purpose designed, and incorporated into each of the houses built or converted for his family by her husband, the architect CH James. Thus he endorsed her professional status and her door was closed upon staff or family when she donned her blue smock and settled to work. CH James practised from four successive offices in WC2 and WC1 and he was affectionately remembered as a delightful egoist. Although his wife co-operated with him on certain projects and they had similar opinions on art and society, their working lives were separate. Calkin James, with significant emphasis, asserted that 'No wife can ever work with a husband at home!!'

Calkin James kept an order book which she had begun in the Rainbow Workshops and maintained throughout her working life. A gap in this book after 1921 signalled her adjustment to family life. It also denoted the forging of her new identity as a designer in the modern industrial era. As well as houses for expanding suburbs and civic buildings for provincial towns, her husband was to design offices and factories for the manufacture and distribution of new consumer goods; these stemmed from scientific advances, new materials, new forms of power and the spread of cars, roads and transport networks for freight, mail and commuters. From America came the notions of marketing management, advertising agencies and the rapid inter-war development of mass advertising. Calkin James adapted to all this without departing from the outlook and disciplines she had adopted at the Central School.

The order book, reopened in 1927, provides a job by job record of the professional life of a freelance designer working in these new commercial and industrial circumstances. Each entry outlined the client, the brief and a deadline for completion or for submitting the rough. Occasionally dimensions were noted or an 'approx. estimate' quoted in guineas. Many jobs entailed preliminary sketches or back-up material but these were systematically disposed of as each job was delivered and a line drawn through the entry. The interchanging roles of agencies, clients and suppliers meant that the same names would reappear under various headings, for example, for a job recorded as 'Kynoch Press' a note was added 'Curwens to do printing'. In another entry with 'Curwen Press' as client, the job was a window bill for the Chelsea Flower Show, ultimately financed by London Transport. This, after 1933, was the new identity of the transport network directed by Frank Pick. Before that 'Underground'

During the early 'twenties Calkin and most of her family embraced the Christian Science religion. This involves a penetration beyond material appearances, seeing matter not as a God-created substance but as a limited mode of human perception. In an increasingly mechanistic cultural climate, her life and work upheld this belief in a spiritual order. Throughout her life she designed, wrote, illustrated and bound small volumes of verse or devotional writings for presentation to family and friends.

An important calligraphic commission, for the Coronation in 1953, was the Loyal Address from the British subjects of the Christian Science Movement presented to Her Majesty The Queen. 517 Christian Science churches and societies were listed in groups under the relevant coats of arms or badges, as researched and depicted by Calkin James. One page is illustrated opposite.

BRITISH GUIANA

Christian Science Society, Georgetown.

HONG KONG

First Church of Christ, Scientist, Hong Kong.

JAMAICA

First Church of Christ, Scientist, Kingston.　　　Second Church of Christ, Scientist, Kingston.

Title page of an unfinished manuscript of the Gospel of St. John. Undated, but probably c.1921. Calkin James rarely left a task uncompleted.

This cover for the Coronation Number of the *Manchester Guardian* in 1937 uses heraldry, symmetry and a serif typeface for a traditional occasion. It is difficult for a post-1945 generation to envisage the hierarchical society between the wars, when Royal Jubilees and Coronations were international occasions of genuine celebration.

Calkin James used similar colours but an asymmetrical layout and sans-serif type to create a modern image for Shell Mex: in this campaign they laid claim to the speed, power and glamour of the new technology.

This colour rough is one of few surviving examples of original artwork by Margaret Calkin James. During holidays at West Wittering in the late 'twenties the James family watched the annual Schneider Trophy taking place off the Isle of Wight.

Two posters of 1932 also serve to illustrate Calkin James's adaptation of style to content. Both had a flatness and immediacy that called attention to their message.

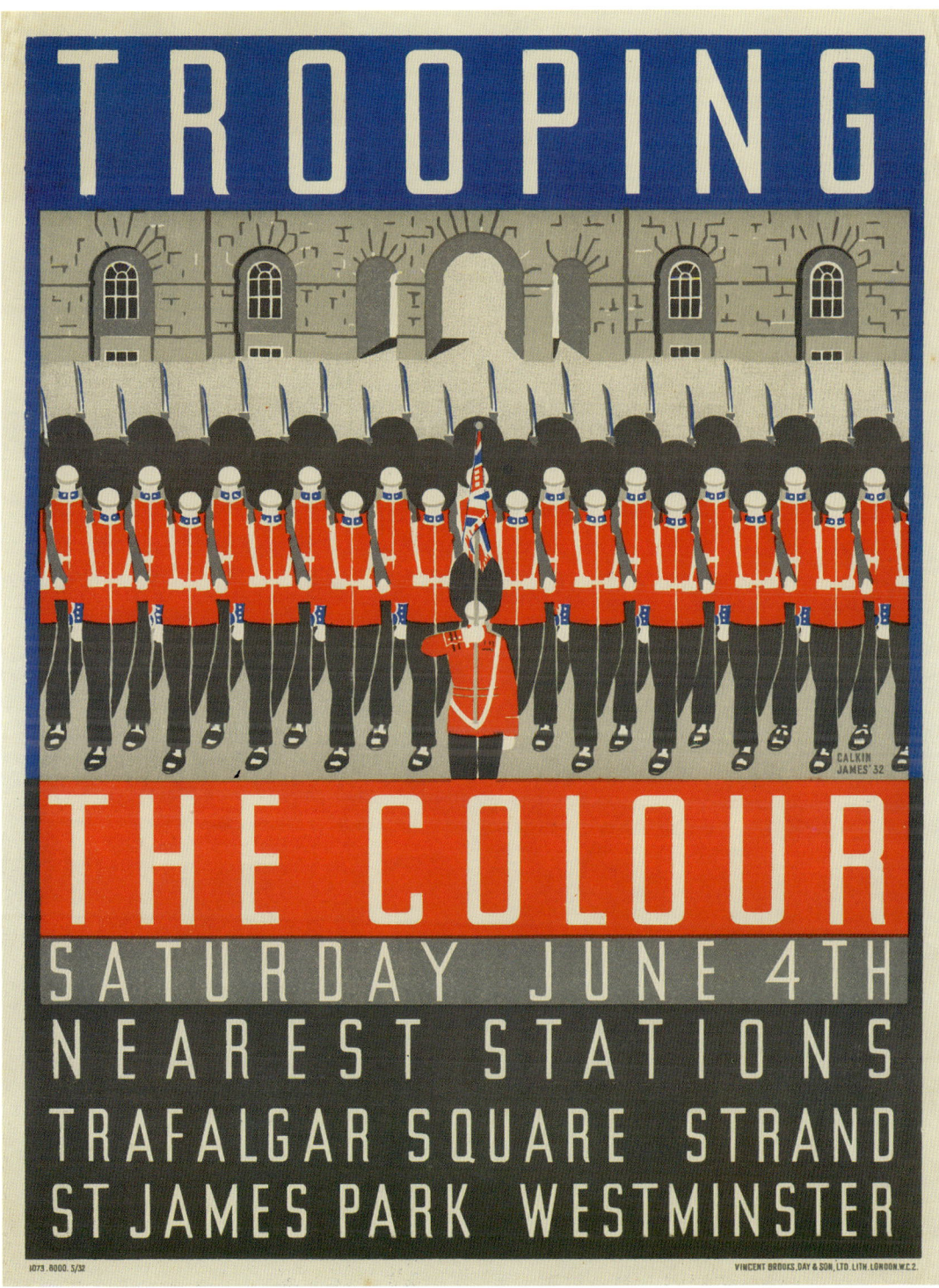

Trooping the Colour had well-drilled rows of vertical soldiers in red on a sober pavement, yet the blue band and the central Union Jack lent an air of pageantry.

A dynamic contrast was the other grand event promoted by Mrs. James that year: the *Royal Tournament*. Here a single image of uniform size was repeated, overlapping, in two rows. So there was no illusion of depth, only a very animated pattern of colour and movement across the surface, denoting the promise of action and excitement, and banners crossed to lead the eye forward. The letters, adapted from classic forms, are tipped forward in agreement with the theme, while those in *Trooping the Colour* stand up straight and tall like soldiers on parade.

Chelsea Flower Show, 1935.

© London Regional Transport.
Courtesy London Transport Museum.

Margaret Calkin James's Order Book entry ran:
Jan. 17th Curwen Press
Design for Chelsea Flower Show
Window Bill L.P.T.B.

The Curwen Press 'Orders and Payments to
Artists 1933 – 41' recorded the completion of
this piece of work on 15.5.35 for a fee of '10gns
nett' which was paid on the 28.5.35.

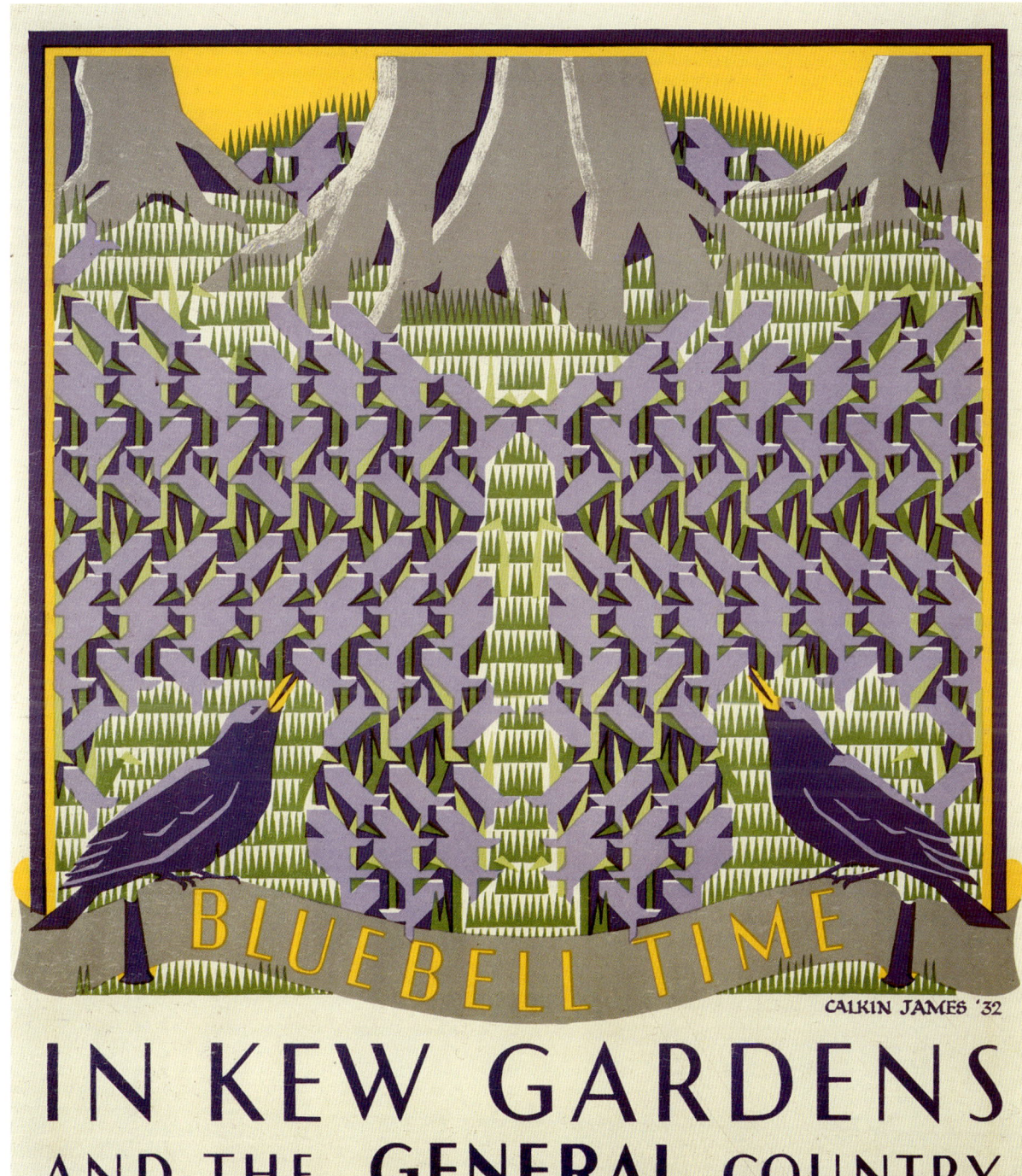

Bluebell Time, 1932.

© London Regional Transport. Courtesy London Transport Museum.

The underground was crowded during rush hours but to encourage people to use the service in their leisure time, posters focused on the marvellous places and events that could be reached by train. *QED* (1929) skilfully incorporated some well-groomed passengers travelling by tube to join the audience for a spectacular West End chorus line-up. This poster could well have been static with its authoritative bold capitals, its strong horizontal bands, the symmetry on a strict geometrical grid and its subdued range of tones. Instead these all combined to make a memorable and lively image.

© London Regional Transport.
Courtesy London Transport Museum.

Posters advertising *Kenwood* and *Box Hill* (both 1935) appealed to the English vein of nostalgia for the leafy rural scene. The sunny landscapes were organised into formal arrangements of flat harmonising colours. These pictures appear conventional nowadays but to the public between the wars they looked decidedly non-naturalistic.

© London Regional Transport.
Courtesy London Transport Museum.

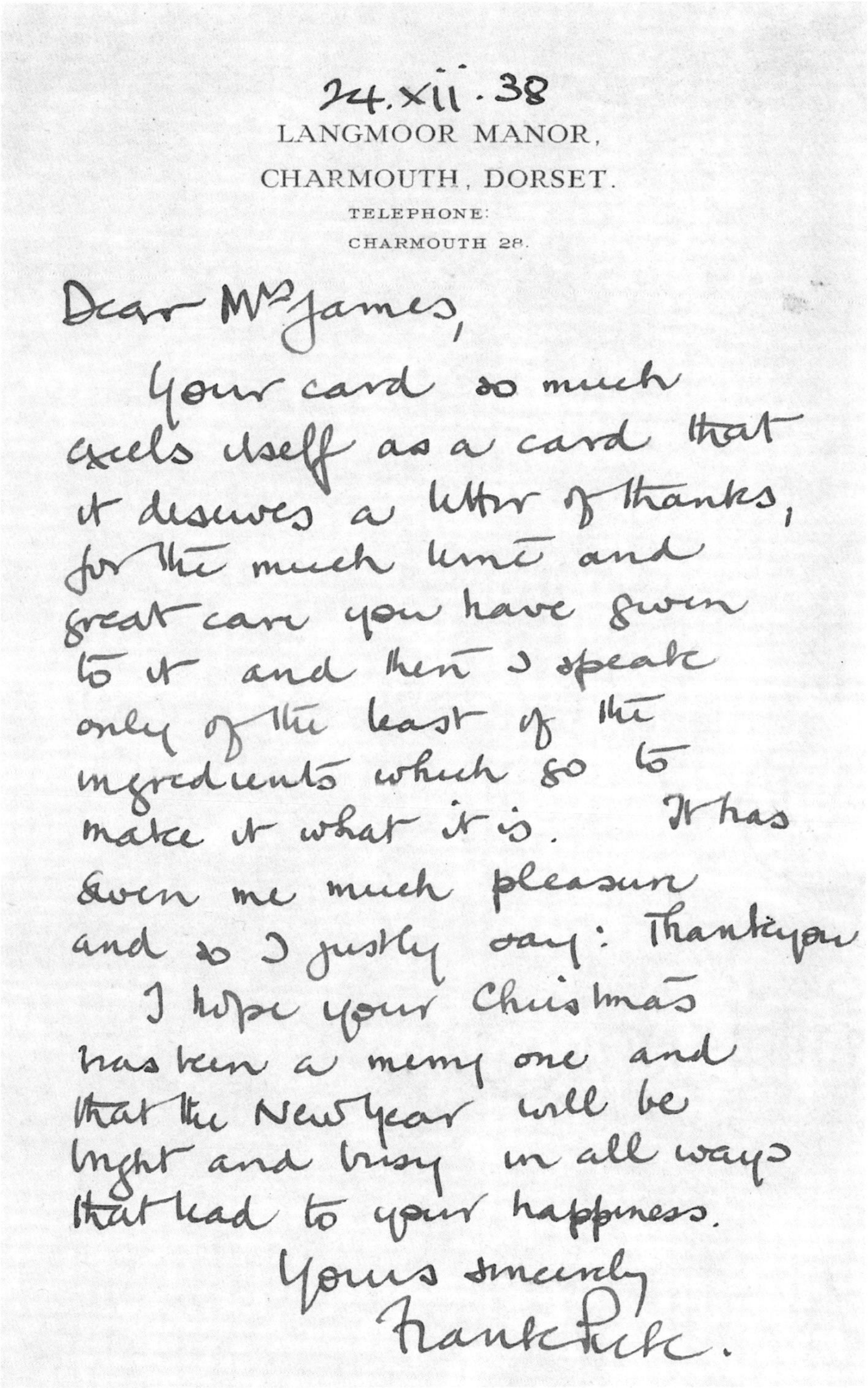

24.xii.38

LANGMOOR MANOR,

CHARMOUTH, DORSET.

TELEPHONE:

CHARMOUTH 28.

Dear Mrs James,

Your card so much excels itself as a card that it deserves a letter of thanks, for the much time and great care you have given to it and then I speak only of the least of the ingredients which so to make it what it is. It has given me much pleasure and so I justly say: Thank you

I hope your Christmas has been a merry one and that the New Year will be bright and busy in all ways that lead to your happiness.

Yours sincerely

Frank Pick.

Letter to Calkin James from Frank Pick, 1938.

Opposite: panel poster for Christmas 1931. Small posters like this could vary in size and shape as they were not displayed in a frame but on the glass screens inside the Underground cars.

© London Regional Transport.
Courtesy London Transport Museum.

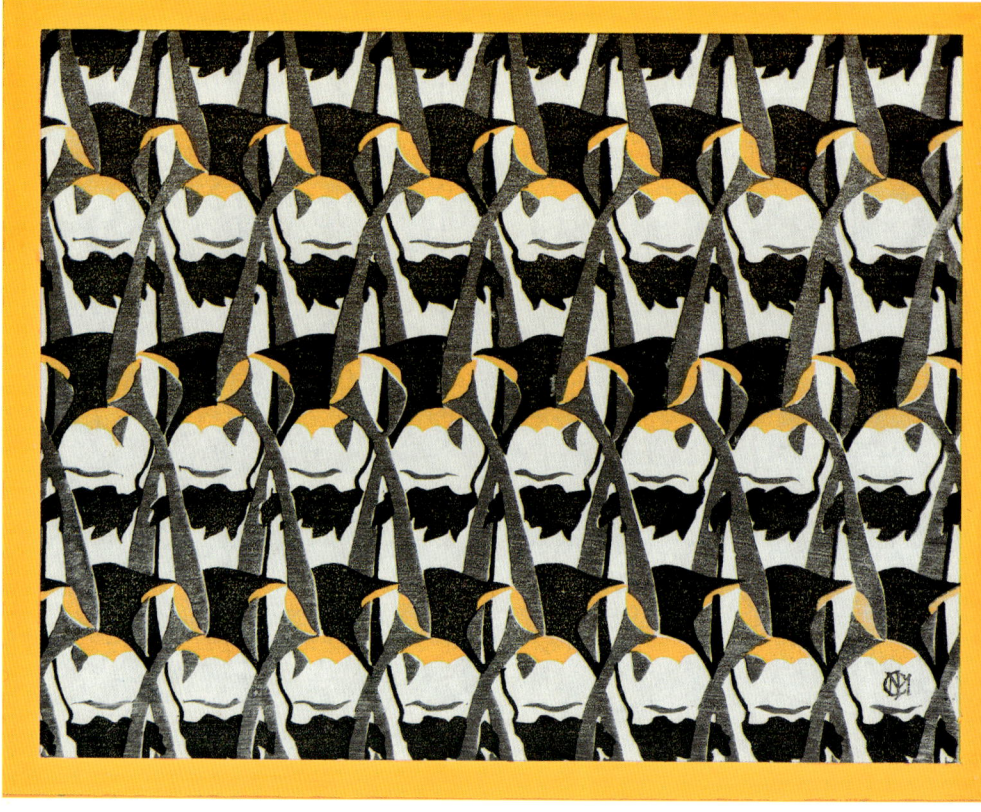

Postcard from CFA Voysey, 1935. Voysey, himself a prolific pattern-maker, especially relished 'the designs and illuminations' in Calkin James's Bond Street exhibition.

Anna Simons, a disciple of Edward Johnston, stressed that his fundamental principles and ideas of construction were liberating to those who applied them afresh to contemporary design briefs: 'I know of no craft which imparts so easily and so perfectly a strong feeling for rhythm, this conspicuous feature of all modern art'. All of Calkin James's work benefitted from her grounding in the revived classical proportions and sound craftsmanship of calligraphy. To these she added her own lively freedom of expression and awareness of new ideas. Her visual and manual skills were subsequently applied across a very wide range of media. In the 'Penguin' linocut, a bird fabric sample, a floral pattern paper and in the interlocking type and keys, she displayed her propensity for pattern-making.

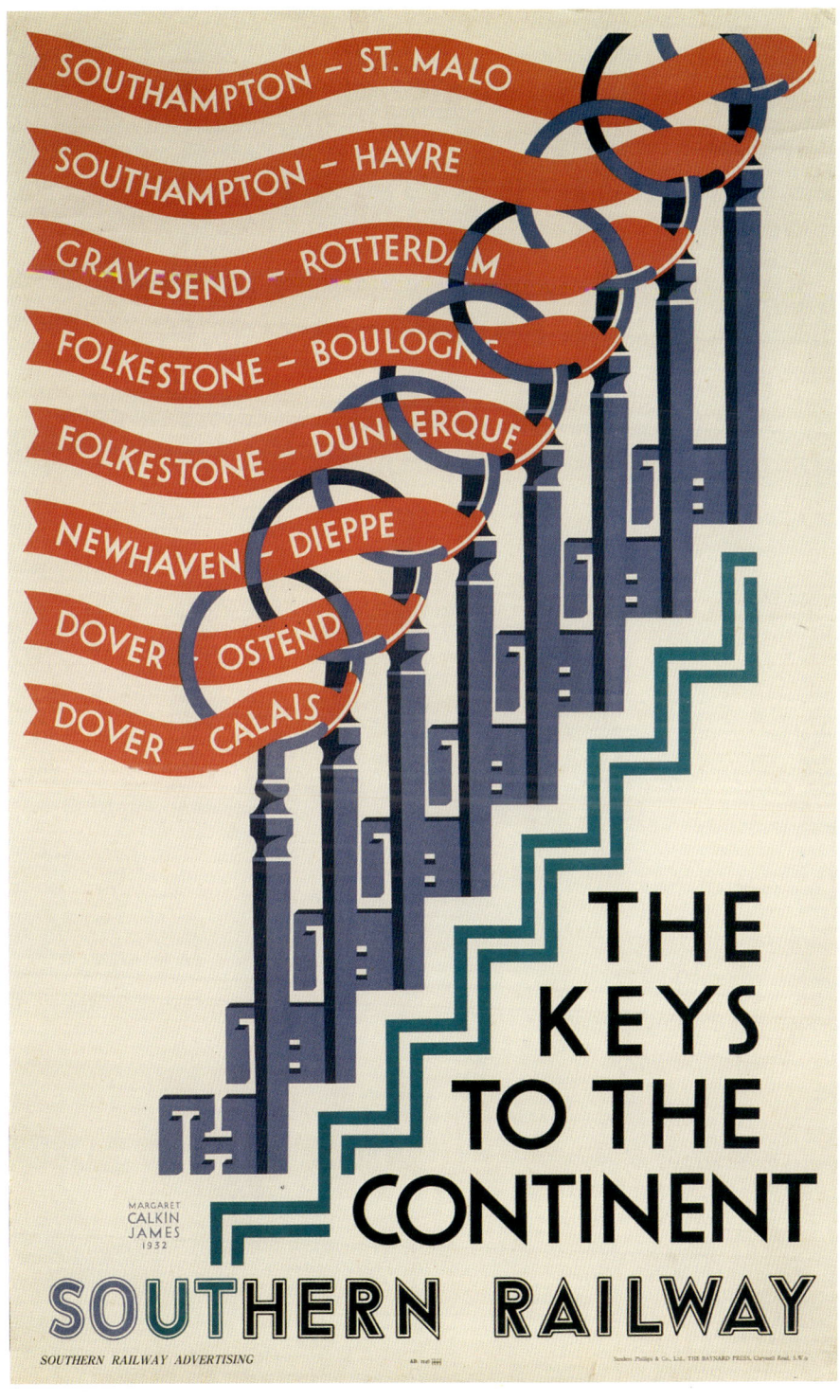

Poster for Southern Railway Advertising designed by Calkin James in 1932 and printed by The Baynard Press.

Spread from *Lettering of Today* (1937) by Anna Simons. A cover by Calkin James was reproduced alongside contemporary examples by such worthies as Berthold Wolpe, Barnett Freeman and Lynton Lamb, each shown as a model for modern designers.

Calkin James designed an alphabet for the cloth covers and jackets of the 'Life and Letters' series for Jonathan Cape, and another for *Juan in America* and *Juan in China*.

The distinctiveness achieved by creating hand-drawn letter-forms to suit the individual character of the title might be augmented by a relevant ornament, a stylised illustration or by a repeating pattern with the title laid out in a superimposed 'box'. These entailed research into history, a knowledge of foreign cultures and the constant discipline of objective drawing.

The BBC booklet for 1929 featured a sober serif type-face, centred and balanced by heraldic devices top and bottom. A strong border pattern of purple thistles and leaves added a light-hearted 'Scottish' flavour. The 1930-31 concert programme for the BBC was equally suited to its theme. The letterforms were distinctly modern and in keeping with the bold, black shapes repeated just enough to suggest an orchestra.

MODERN CHINESE CIVILIZATION
BY
DR. A. F. LEGENDRE
TRANSLATED FROM THE FRENCH BY
ELSIE MARTIN JONES

A WINDOW DICTIONARY
*
W. F. Crittall

BROADCASTS *for* SCOTTISH SCHOOLS

PROGRAMME
JANUARY—JUNE 1929
SYLLABUS
JANUARY 14th—MARCH 22nd, 1929

BRITISH BROADCASTING CORPORATION

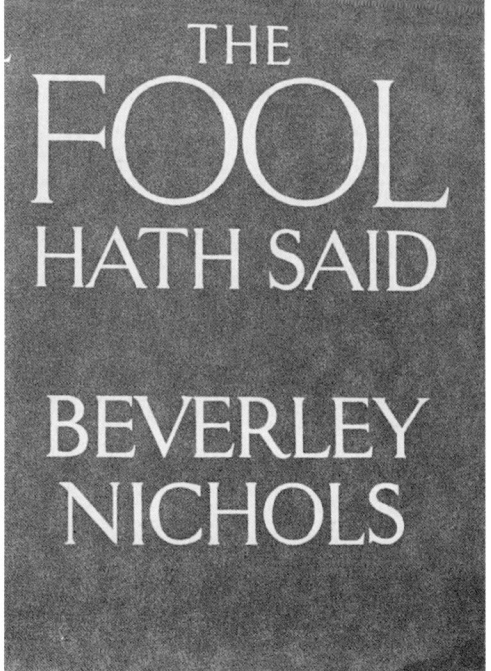

THE FOOL HATH SAID
BEVERLEY NICHOLS

BEN JONSON
&KING JAMES
BY ERIC LINKLATER
AUTHOR OF
'JUAN IN AMERICA'

B.B.C SYMPHONY CONCERTS
SEASON 1930·31

SERIES 'B'
THE BRITISH BROADCASTING CORPORATION
PROGRAMME, WEDNESDAY, 29 OCTOBER
Price one shilling

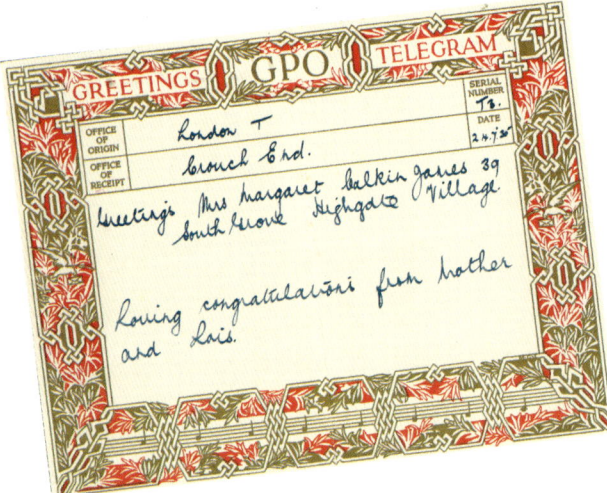

In 1935 Sir Stephen Tallents commissioned Calkin James to design the first of the new General Post Office Greetings Telegrams. These quickly became popular and later designs were commissioned from Edward Ardizzone, John Farleigh, Barnett Freedman and Robert Gibbings. Sir Stephen sent Calkin James a sample of the handbill she had also designed to announce the new service in 'some 23,000 post offices all over the U.K. tomorrow morning', adding in an accompanying personal note that she 'deserved' to have a copy.

By 1935 the GPO had established a standard range of coloured telephones: chinese red, ivory, jade green and black. Calkin James designed a poster to urge the public to 'consider your colour scheme'. In another poster design she managed to unite all four colour options in one image by the artful use of the same background drapery in different colourways to match each phone.

Opposite: Book covers designed by Calkin James for Jonathan Cape.

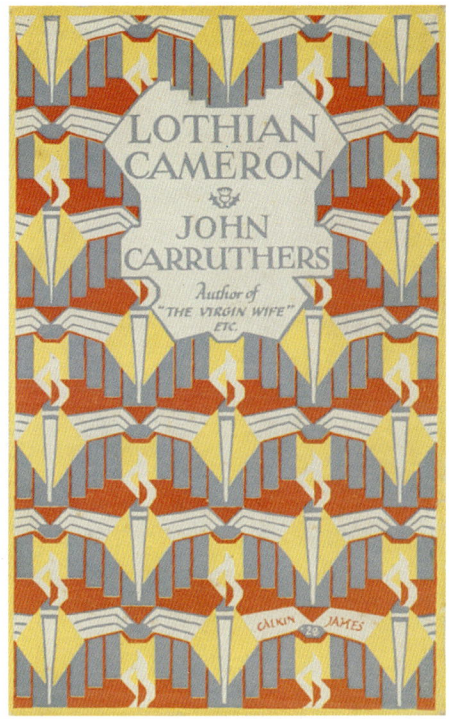

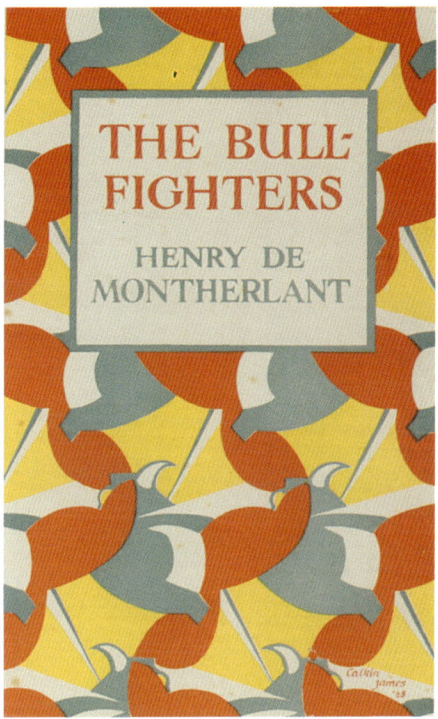

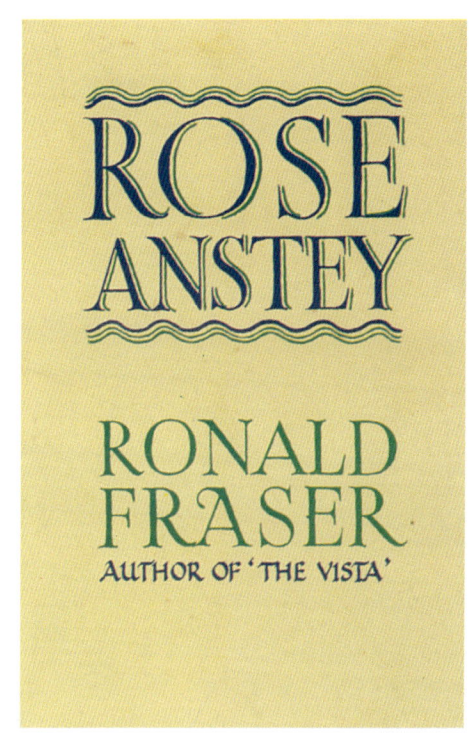

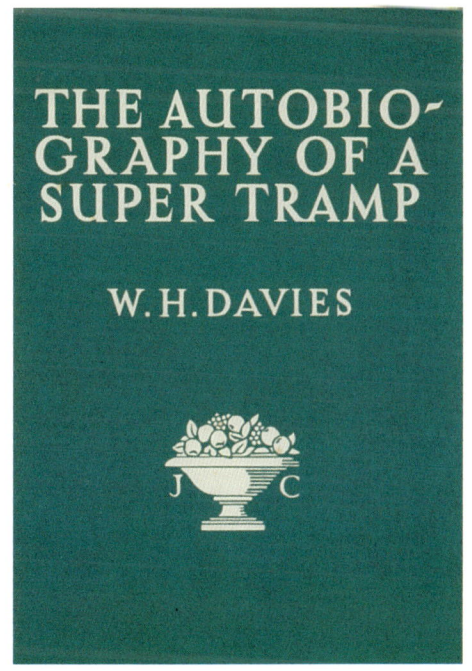

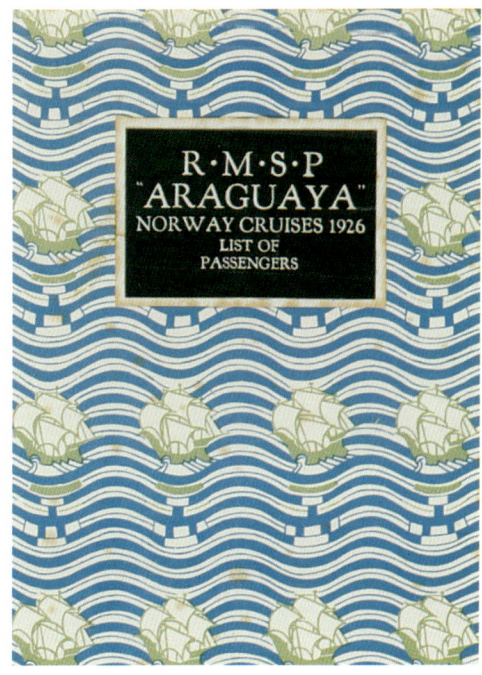

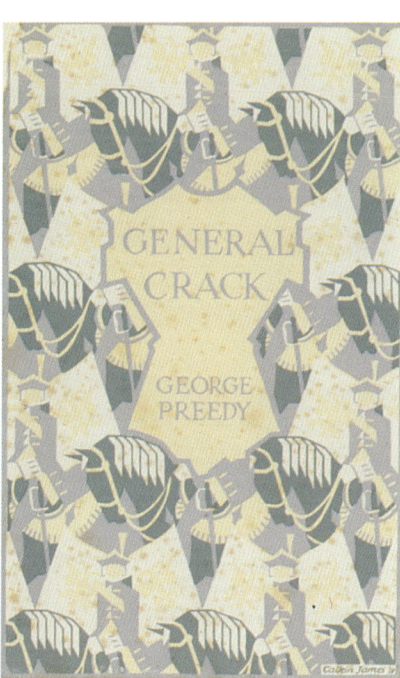

Room converted into a studio for Calkin James at South Grove, Highgate, 1934. The settee was a plan chest covered with a Heal's mattress, ending in a rounded cocktail cabinet. The floor was covered with large plywood squares stained silver grey and the folding doors simplified by covering them with plywood. The curtains bear a large leaf pattern in the style of Marion Dorn which sits happily enough with the Persian rug; the streamlined modernity of the fixtures and fittings also blends comfortably with what was retained of the 18th century – the proportions of the room, the cornice and the pattern of the glazing bars.

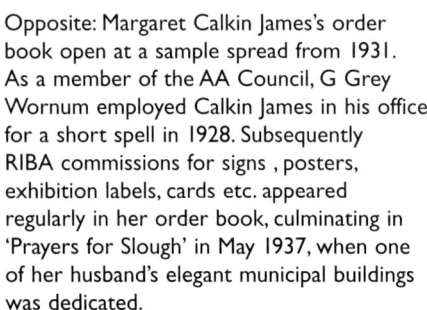

Opposite: Margaret Calkin James's order book open at a sample spread from 1931. As a member of the AA Council, G Grey Wornum employed Calkin James in his office for a short spell in 1928. Subsequently RIBA commissions for signs, posters, exhibition labels, cards etc. appeared regularly in her order book, culminating in 'Prayers for Slough' in May 1937, when one of her husband's elegant municipal buildings was dedicated.

frequently cropped up as a client. Initially she dealt with a Mr Patmore, though by 1928 it was Pick who exclaimed 'Impossible!' when her husband delivered a job on her behalf because she was giving birth to her third child.

In the early years of this century no one could be unaware of the dynamic modern movements affecting all the arts. Edward McKnight Kauffer's radical innovations and genius for self-publicity did much to boost the reputation of the design profession. As a Vorticist he had used abstraction in poster designs, hoping, like the Italian Futurists, to create dynamic symbols of optimism for post-war reconstruction and a new era of equal opportunity. At the same time he delighted in reclaiming earlier forms of graphic communication. The young Calkin's illustrated handbills for the *Cautionary Tales* were reminiscent of a fashionable revival of traditional broadside ballad sheets, chap books, old printers' flowers and traditional type designs. In 1920 Kauffer's paintings were exhibited with former Vorticists such as Wyndham Lewis at the Mansard Gallery in Heals, Tottenham Court Road, not far from Calkin's Rainbow Workshops in Great Russell Street. It is no surprise to discover that his

10

Oct. 3rd   The Rev. L. S. Hunter
Memorial in book form to The Marories
of Barking.

Oct. 15th.   B. B. C. Design for
Symphony Concert Programme.

Nov.   R. I. B. A. Labels &
                posters

Dec. 20   Feather Jackets for L. o. Letters
Series.   Nos. 16 & 21
                1931

Jan. 5.   R. I. B. A. labels & 2 posters
for Annual Prizes & Scholarships
                £ 2. 10. 0

Jan 27th   R. I. B. A. 2 labels &
2 posters   15/

Jan. 28th   Jonathan Cape. Ltd
Lettered Jacket for "The Apostate"
2 lots on buff paper.

Jan 28th   R. I. B. A. "Smoking"
cards (6) £7. 5. 0   + framing

Feb. 10th   Jonathan Cape Ltd
Jacket for Pyramid & Temple.

Feb. 10th   R. I. B. A.
Exhibition of Architectural Travel
Posters 2 Posters 1 label for Col. posters
1 List

11.

Feb. 28th   R. I. B. A.
2 Posters 1 label   9 ft × 30"
"The Works of Sir Edwin Cooper"
Paper 1/6   £1-2-6

March 2nd   Jonathan Cape.
Press announcement for "Juan
in America   1 guinea.

March 5th   L. L. Series "Brontë Sisters"

March.   Jonathan Cape
"Adventures of Rashleigh"

April 10. "Passages from Arabia Deserta"

April 16   R. I. B. A
"Exhibition of Modern Transport.
14. 10 ft labels in pen lettering
2 notices 'To the Exhibition' Romans
1 Poster.   34 hrs.   £8. 10. 0
Paper Ink card   £ 1 - 0 - 0
                £ 9. 10. 0

April 24.   Ilford Ltd.
2 Designs for cover of tin for
Panchromatic Cine Films.

May 7th   Institution of Mechanical
Engineers   Address in English & German

Two pattern papers by Calkin James from *A Specimen Book of Pattern Papers designed for and in use at the Curwen Press*, Introduction by Paul Nash, Fleuron Ltd, 1928.

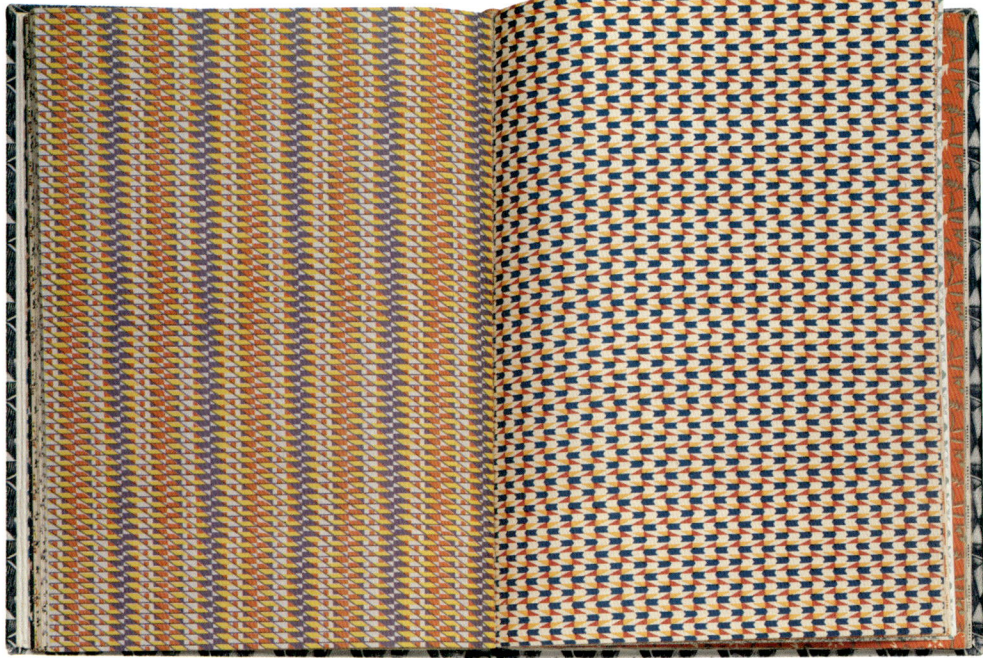

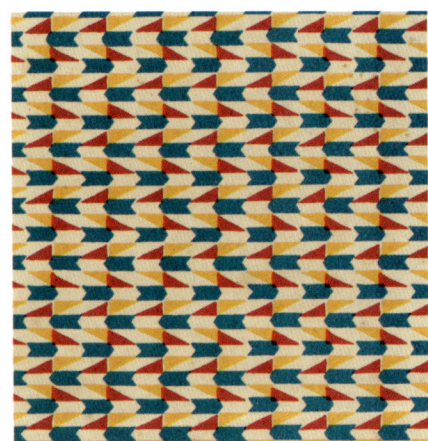

Calkin James designed the first pattern paper for the Curwen Press in 1922. It was a tiny, overall geometric pattern in clear bright colours and was reprinted many times. Imprecise technical notes on the colours used to print these decorative papers depended on human judgment when mixing ink – 'sienna with a dash of ochre' – so that samples from different printings could and did vary! Many more pattern paper commissions in abstract or small floral patterns ensued. One is illustrated opposite at actual size.

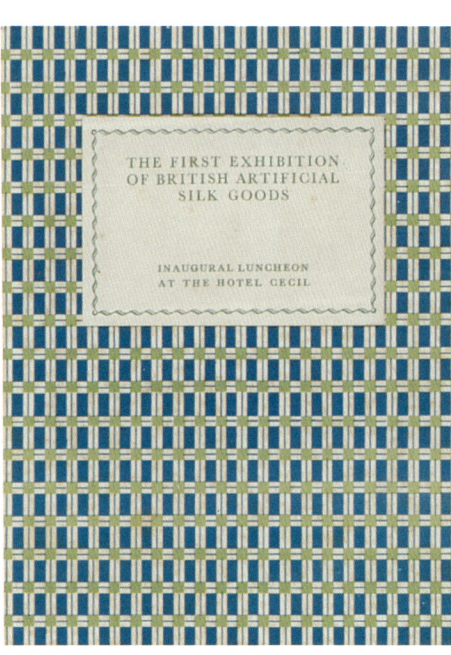

THE FIRST EXHIBITION
OF BRITISH ARTIFICIAL
SILK GOODS

INAUGURAL LUNCHEON
AT THE HOTEL CECIL

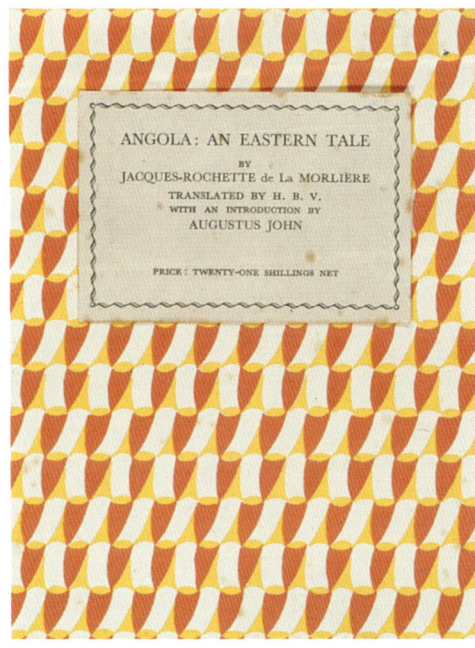

ANGOLA: AN EASTERN TALE
BY
JACQUES-ROCHETTE de La MORLIÈRE
TRANSLATED BY H. B. V.
WITH AN INTRODUCTION BY
AUGUSTUS JOHN

PRICE: TWENTY-ONE SHILLINGS NET

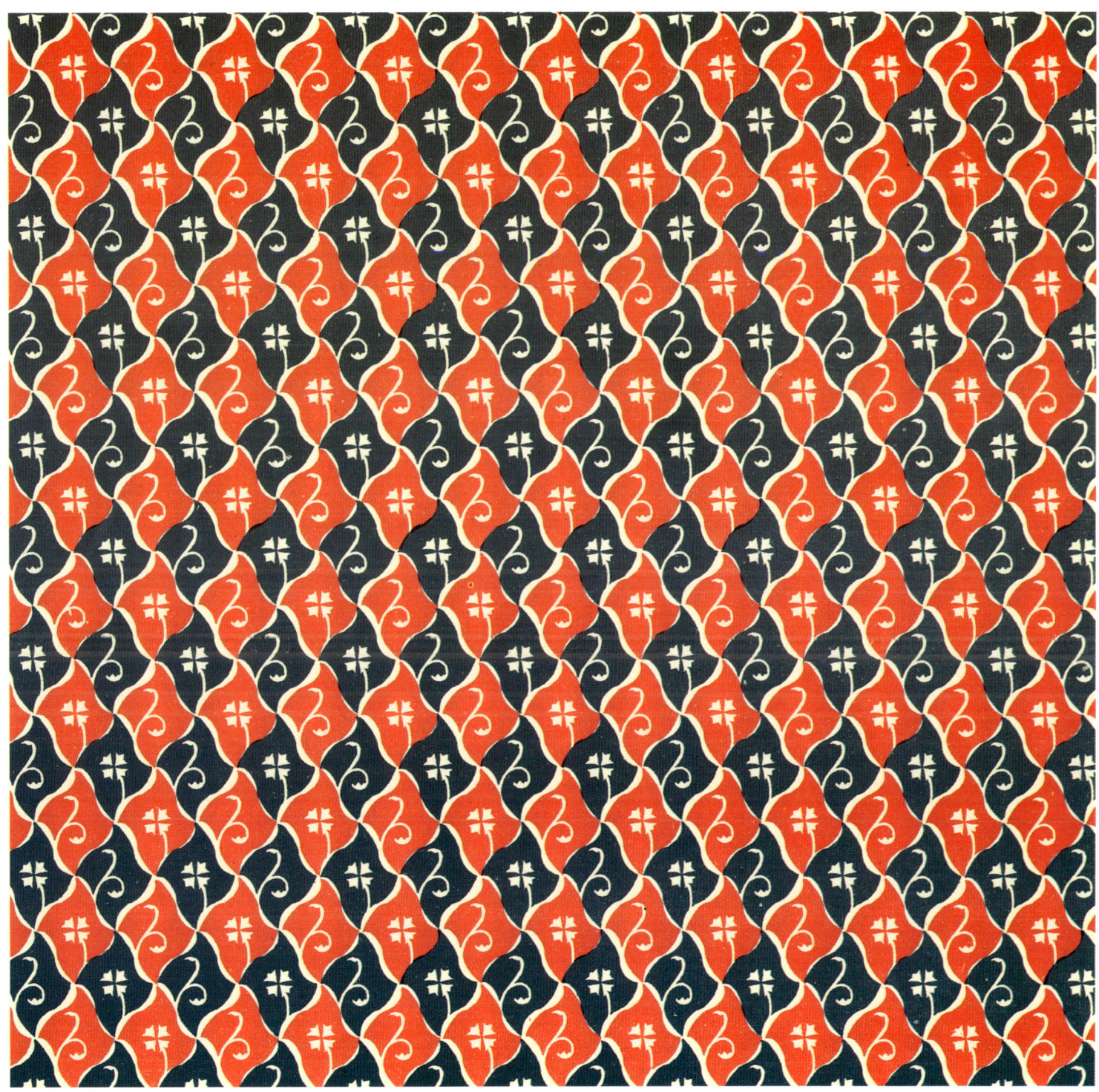

influence was even more direct: her *QED* poster for London Underground was accorded a full-page reproduction in *Commercial Art*, October 1928, to demonstrate the effectiveness of Kauffer's tuition in poster design at the Westminster School of Art. His blending of old stability with new devices like symbolism and geometric flatness were very much in line with Calkin's own thinking.

Poster designs by avant-garde artists, or reflecting fine art trends, were part of a new marketing drive led by DIA enthusiasts like Frank Pick. One of the boldest pioneers of new styles in advertising, Pick was the publicity manager of London Underground. Convinced of the link between aesthetic quality and commercial effectiveness, he established a high standard of design throughout the network in stations, rolling stock and facilities. Pick's boldness in employing the well-known artists of the day earned the tube platform the title of 'the poor man's picture gallery', just as Wyndham Lewis had predicted.

Within these sweeping policies Pick allowed designers a very free hand and often the results did not even directly refer to transport themes. Pick wanted people to use the service in their leisure time and not only during rush hours when the Underground was crowded. So posters focused on the marvellous places and events that could be reached by train. *QED* shows Pick's willingness to give the artist an open brief: Calkin James originated the concept of this poster as well as its design and artwork. *Quod erat demonstrandum* was a familiar latin tag for schoolchildren demonstrating that a tricky mathematical problem had been solved. Here the evident conclusion to be drawn was that the well-groomed audience and the members of the spectacular chorus line-up would all travel to the West End by tube.

Pick ensured that his designers had the back up of excellent printing: firms like Waterlows, the Dangerfield Printing Company Limited, the Baynard Press and the Curwen Press all provided a high quality service. Mrs James's contact with the Curwen Press led to miscellaneous smaller jobs such as some lively postcards for Barrows Stores in Birmingham (1937) which represent groceries and how they can be enjoyed.

During the 1920s Pick was also on the committee of the Empire Marketing Board, under Sir Stephen Tallents, who shared Pick's belief that good design meant good business. In 1933 Tallents was transferred to become the first Public Relations Officer of the General Post Office. Jack Beddington of Shell Mex was another DIA associate who was prepared to take risks in his nation-wide publicity campaigns. All these clients appeared regularly in Calkin James's order book. Through the hoardings the conservative British public became visually adjusted to the formal devices that had first appeared in the paintings of Cézanne, the Cubists, the Vorticists and the Futurists, though it did not happen all at once. The man in the street found even a poster like Calkin's *Kenwood* exceedingly 'modern'. While patrician arbiters of public taste like Sir Kenneth Clark applauded the work of the new corporate patrons of artists, it must be remembered that the taste of the majority of marketing men in Britain was still for banal illustration and fussy typography.

Advertising agencies employed teams of in-house designers, but though some jobs were recorded in the order book under Stuarts, APM or Regent Advertising Services, Calkin James had no regular commitment and usually worked directly for clients. However, despite close contact with those who commissioned their work, designers were, as far as the public was concerned, a largely anonymous service. In a promotional brochure of 1921 the Curwen Press professed to 'work in friendly co-operation with a wide range of independent designers who liked to help the Press... the Press in return does not desire the designer to be unknown but recognises him as a valuable co-worker.' In 1922 the Curwen Press launched their printed pattern papers with an edition of 475 sheets of Calkin James's *Harlequin*, soon to be reprinted as it proved popular with publishers and bookbinders. By 1938, more than 24,000 sheets had been printed but Calkin James's name was never added (though papers by Edward Bawden, Harold Jones and others did bear the artists' names in a self-conscious bid by Curwen to build up the mythology of the Press and bolster up certain artists.) Another pattern was issued in 1927 and her fee was £3-15s-7d. There was no further remuneration though it, too, was in print for several decades. But if copyright laws concerning royalties or repeat fees had been in force, the Curwen Press would not have been willing to risk imaginative ventures like these papers.

Taken on their own, Calkin James's posters could be slotted into a Modernist framework, but they were only one aspect of her work and she did not impose any such agenda willy-nilly. Instead she adapted her style to suit each commission. In a poster like *Bluebell Time* she transformed the delicate observations of her water-colour studies into flat patterns, sharp contrasts and repetitive forms for instant impact, while her 1937 cover for the Coronation Number of the *Manchester Guardian* is a more formal piece of heraldry for a traditional occasion. Lettering and imagery were similarly suited to subject matter for the BBC programme covers of 1929 and 1930.

Watercolour, 1943
Rickyard at Lapstone Farm, Chipping Camden,
where the James family lived from 1939 to
1942.

Watercolour, 1943. View from Dover's Hill,
Chipping Camden, over the Vale of Evesham.

She carried on her painting in conjunction with her commissioned work, but did not attempt to depict the everyday stresses of city life or modernity. Instead she chose to paint domestic scenes or rural landscapes in a straight-forward, documentary style betraying no hint of mysticism, surrealism or abstraction. Sensitivity and truthfulness was also apparent in her flower studies. She delighted in the variety and richness of plants and a strong feeling for structure precluded any hint of academic dullness. 'Freshness, economy of means and a quite remarkable purity of colour' were the hallmarks of her painting technique, as noted in a *Times* review of her 1935 exhibition at the Cooling Galleries in New Bond Street. In 1948 she had an exhibition at Kensington Art Gallery and a further exhibition in 1957 in St George's Gallery, Cork Street.

Marriage to CH James consolidated Calkin James's links with the world of establishment architects and artists. James, like his early masters Sir Edwin Lutyens and then Barry Parker and Raymond Unwin, was an Associate of the Royal Academy of Arts and a regular exhibitor in their annual Summer Exhibition, becoming a Royal Academician in 1947. To Herbert Read and other proponents of Modernism, the RA epitomised the shackles of a dead tradition – they wanted to be done with British sentimentality and nostalgia for the past and hurry into the new machine aesthetic. In reality the Academy had far more success between the wars than Read or the DIA had in 'keeping in touch with the interests and perceptions of ordinary people.' Sir William Llewellyn PRA, wrote in 1935 that the role of the Royal Academy was to foster 'a living and growing tradition' while acting as 'a steadying influence on the exuberance or haste of innovators'.

The Jameses worked in the context of a capital city but both retained an essentially rural frame of mind; CH James loved cricket and the music of Elgar and his wife, writing in 1944 of obtaining a wartime sketching permit for the Norfolk Broads, added 'but one never loses sight of occasional red roofs and I never feel we are in real country'. At this time Calkin James was working on a collection of flower studies to be published together with an anthology of verse. Her selected authors were either concerned with a spiritual quest or with evocations of rural life, for example 'some wizard quotes from Vita Sackville-West's poems especially *The Land*. ... I have also got hold of the *Collected Poems of Mary Webb...* '

Britain in the 'thirties was faced with a slump and massive unemployment. With minimal government funding but much DIA enthusiasm the Council for

Colour linoprint of 'Mermaid' rose, exhibited in the Summer Exhibition, Royal Academy of Arts, 1968.

Art and Industry was established in 1934, chaired by the energetic Frank Pick. Publications were issued and exhibitions organised, to ensure that consumers, designers and manufacturers would all be educated in design matters. Planning and communal effort was also advocated by Walter Gropius, former director of the Bauhaus, who arrived in England in the same year. This was to be extended to all the areas of craft, design, art and architecture. Progressive thinkers like Gropius railed against the 'costly and depraved standards' set by the British Art in Industry Exhibition at the Royal Academy in 1935. In an otherwise scathing *Listener* review, Herbert Read grudgingly allowed that the display of printing and book production – which included several of Calkin James's bookcovers – was 'representative of the fairly high standard which prevails in this industry'

The DIA pundits recognized that German style efficiency was needed in the 'thirties to update British mass-produced goods, just as in 1915 they had looked to the German Werkbund for standards of function, fitness for purpose, truth to materials and economy of means. All of these slogans would have a

Watercolour of rhododendron
'Pink Pearl' painted at
Cannon Cottage, Hampstead
c. 1957.

Opposite: Watercolour of
columbines and doll, 'Ming', who
was purchased for 5 shillings at the
Caledonian Market in 1938, and
dressed in clothes made by
Margaret Calkin James.

familiar ring to Calkin James, since the Germans in the first place had admired these very qualities in the British Arts and Crafts movement. In 1937 the Council for Art and Industry suggested a National Register of Industrial Art Designers, which was duly implemented by the Board of Trade. Anthony Bertram trumpeted this in his BBC radio broadcasts, putting a high premium on originality and creative ability: 'Adapters and copyists need not apply'. Margaret Calkin James was registered at an early stage.

The pattern of privileged male exclusivity so long taken for granted in British society was typically manifested in the Double Crown Club, formed in 1924 by Oliver Simon and Hubert Foss. The James's next-door neighbour in Hampstead Way, G Wren Howard, partner of the publisher Jonathan Cape, was one of 40 founder members who planned to dine together at regular intervals to discuss and maintain high standards of book design and production. Many members of this club were engaged in similar work to Calkin James, for the same clients, but women were not considered for membership, just as they were not able to join the Arts Club. Members could bring guests on Wednesday evenings, and on certain exceptionally grand occasions, so now and then CH James brought his wife and, in later years, his daughters. CFA Voysey's card sending 'sincere congratulations' on Calkin James's 'splendid exhibition' of 1935 was naturally addressed to his Arts Club crony, CH James Esq, and not to the artist herself.

At Jonathan Cape, G Wren Howard was responsible for the appearance and production of the firm's publications. Calkin James's work over two decades measured up to his high standards of craftsmanship and design and also those of John Lane at the Bodley Head. She designed lettering and layouts for their books as well as labels, leaflets, press advertisements and showcards. All displayed the characteristics of the English typographic reform inspired at first by William Morris and subsequently by the private presses at the beginning of the twentieth century. Legibility was the fundamental requirement, but Calkin James often enhanced the book title with written scripts, flourishes, ornaments or stylised illustrations. To draw the eye and hold the interest can, on the other hand, be a very subtle and quiet art using well spaced lettering and careful layout alone. Her aim, learned from Edward Johnson, was always to make good letters and to arrange them well.

CH James shared with his wife the convictions of William Morris and WR Lethaby that art should be wedded to morality, politics and religion. Lethaby's conception of a modernism built on tradition was frequently echoed

NATIONAL REGISTER
OF INDUSTRIAL ART DESIGNERS

This is to certify that

Margaret Bernard Calkin James

has been registered as a qualified designer
for Industry

DATE   January 1938
        valid for Three years

                                    C Tennyson
                                            Chairman

                                    T R Ferguson
                                            Registrar

National Register of Industrial Art Designers
certificate 1938.

in CH James's early lectures to the Architectural Association and In his publications. Good architecture was not necessarily a matter of originality or newness, it was 'more frequently merely the development of old ideas to suit new conditions.' Soundness of construction, honesty to materials and suitability to the individual locality could all be achieved in even the very simplest of groups, though he would brook no economies at the expense of 'reasonable permanence'. He was well aware of conditions in the wake of the First World War: a severe shortage of houses, a slum clearance problem and the vital factor of minimum cost.

CH James showed a special ingenuity in the planning of 'small houses'. They were not usually so small as to exclude accommodation for the maid. The inclusion of servants' accommodation in their own houses was as important as the provision of a studio for Calkin James, since without domestic help it would have been impossible for her to continue with her freelance work. As a rule they had a cook and a governess (often a European refugee) and occasionally they also employed a 'house parlour man'. Even in the worst years of the Slump

Volume of original watercolours, bound together with hand-written poems in 1970.

During the Second World War, Calkin James began working on this collection of flower studies, to be published together with a poetry anthology. A great deal of research went into finding (or even writing) suitable verses. Her selected authors were either concerned with a spiritual quest or with evocations of rural life. She revelled in the discovery of "some wizard quotes from Vita Sackville-West's poems especially *The Land*" and "the Collected Poems of Mary Webb." In the austerity of the post-war period publishers were unwilling to risk the expense of reproducing such a book.

Margaret Calkin James kept a book of her printed samples and dye recipes from 1936 until 1950. This spread shows how she developed her watercolour studies of favourite flowers into repeating patterns for textiles.

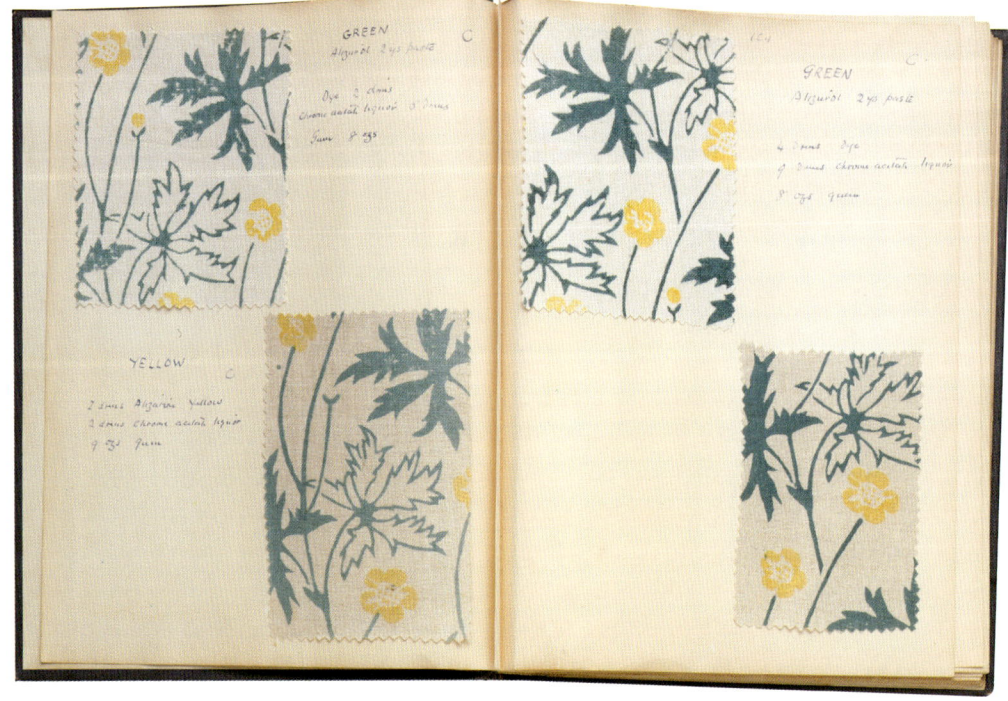

Linoprint of Cyclamen, exhibited in the Summer Exhibition, Royal Academy of Arts, 1965.

there was always at least one servant living in, because Mrs James's income was all the more necessary at a time when architects could find very little employment. Widowed in the early 'fifties, Calkin James moved to Cannon Cottage in Hampstead, where she painted a *trompe l'oeil* 18th-century window plus servant on the plain brick wall at the back: ruefully she declared that the window and equally the maid looking out were now 'wishful thinking'. This window mural (now only faintly visible) was like many of the decorative designs undertaken after her marriage, for her own home. The painted relief of the ark and the rainbow survives above the front door of No. 1 Hampstead Way. Calkin James restored this piece in the 1950s, but the beachscape mural in the bathroom of 39 South Grove, with its sand dunes and pink and white striped bathing tent, was painted out and the wrought iron panel of family initials that once surmounted the back garden door of 'Hornbeams' has disappeared. 'Orthodox histories of design', wrote Helen Rees, 'mirror social convention by confining its study to the professional realm, so that domestic or unpaid work is automatically off limits'.

Painted iron panel showing the family initials above the back door of 'Hornbeams'.

1 Hampstead Way, their first home in Hampstead Garden Suburb, was a simple and compact 3-bedroomed house designed by CH James. Calkin James's workroom, 30 feet long, occupyied the whole of the roof space. The house is a model of economy in planning and the up-to-the-minute labour-saving devices. The growing family moved in 1929 to Fairway House, planned by CH James as one of a group in Fairway Close, Wildwood Road, NW11. This house, with Calkin James's pleasant ground floor studio overlooking the garden, was sold during the Depression.

In 1934 CH James was praised in the architectural press for the admirably restrained conversion of an adjoining pair of nineteenth-century houses in South Grove, Highgate, one of which became their home for the next two years. The room converted into a studio for Calkin James was photographed by Dell and Wainwright (famous for creating many striking images of Modernist buildings for *Architectural Review* between the Wars).

Finally CH James was able to build his showpiece, 'Hornbeams', in Winnington Road, N2. The family lived there for three years until it was requisitioned in 1939, returned in 1945 and remained there until CH James died in 1953. 'Hornbeams' was featured in the architectural press as a striking example of an architect's house, illustrating his attention to detail and choice of quality building materials. Here again the studio, next to the large living room, opened onto the back garden. 'Hornbeams' gave both the Jameses an

Trompe l'oeil mural on exterior plain brick wall by Margaret Calkin James, *c.*1955. Calkin James's last home in Hampstead was Cannon Cottage in Well Road, built in 1702. There was no window on the back wall, so she prepared an 8 by 4 foot surface and painted a window with an eighteenth-century maidservant looking out over a window box.

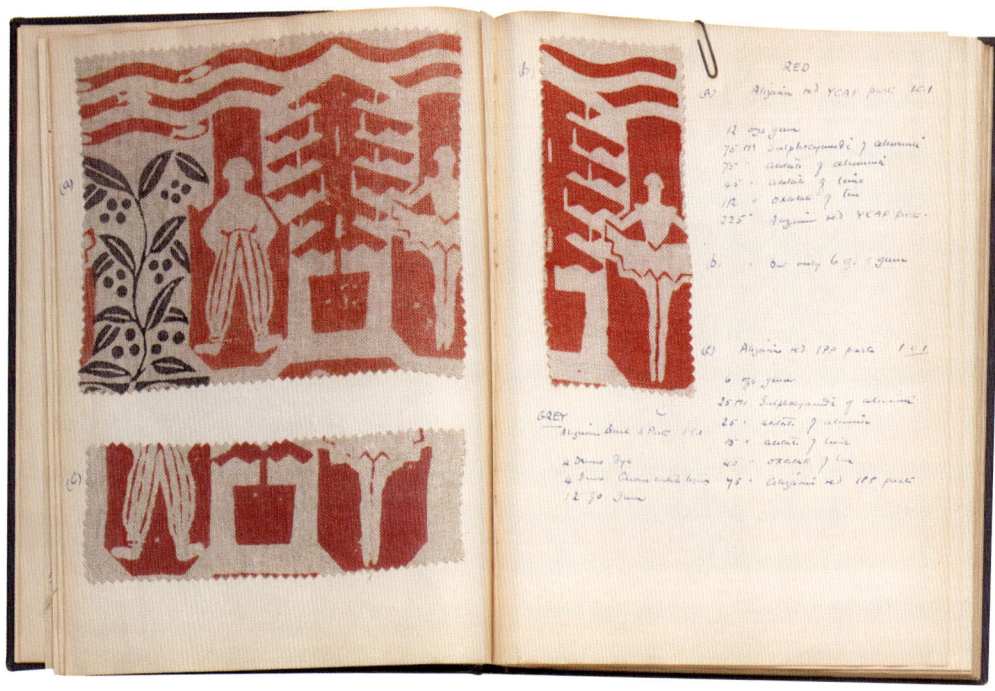

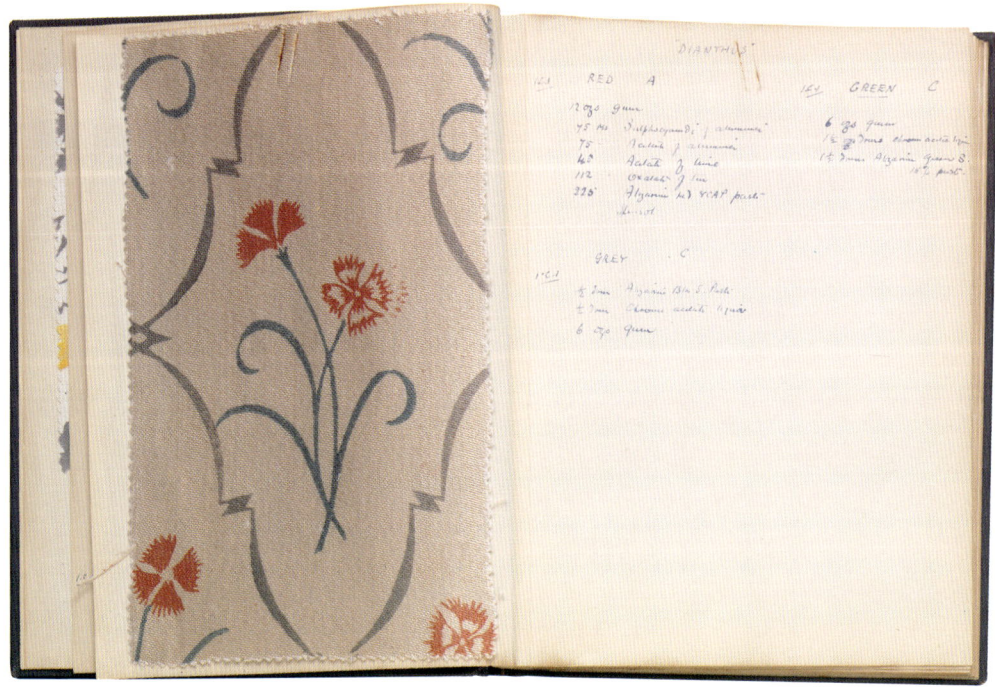

Sample book of woodblock designs for fabric printing, with notes of dye recipes. The top spread shows the schoolroom fabric, which incorporated many of Calkin James's favourite motifs, including the ark and rainbow.

Opposite:
Woodblock-printed curtain fabric, 1936. Designed and handprinted on linen by Margaret Calkin James for the children's schoolroom at 'Hornbeams', the family home in Hampstead Garden Suburb designed by CH James.

Margaret Calkin James and her first child, Brian, seated near the trellis at 1 Hampstead Way, 1923.

opportunity to carry out their personal preferences for traditional craftsmanship and materials. As well as the soft furnishings hand block-printed by Calkin James, the children's bathroom was 'pleasantly tiled in lemon, white and grey, to her design. There were also dining and sitting rooms and kitchen; open-plan living was not favoured by CH James.

On one previous occasion, 5 October 1932, Calkin James's order book records a commission from the Edinburgh Weavers for 'Designs for woven and printed fabric repeats'. Apart from this, all her fabric designs were for 'Hornbeams' and she printed them there single-handed. The cutting of wooden blocks, the mixing of dyes (and mordants when needed), the dyeing process, followed by steaming and lengthy washings, rinsings and ironing all amounted to an arduous performance. She used a galvanised dustbin for steaming and a rudimentary gas ring for heating the dye. Quite apart from the physical labour, much research into recipes and methods was required. As Susan Bosence points out, the techniques and ideals of other countries and of previous centuries are nowadays well-documented, 'but those pioneers in the 'twenties and 'thirties had to find things out for themselves.'

The methodical 'house-keeping' of her order book can also be observed in her sample book of woodblock designs for fabric printing. Pattern samples in various colour options were pasted next to dye recipes; though they were designed and printed in her home for private family use, she brought her customary professionalism to bear.

CH James was included in John Betjeman's list of architects of the 1920s who looked to the past and to developments abroad to escape from Edwardian vulgarity. With his usual twinkle Betjeman described them as 'masters of a new restrained style springing from late Georgian and late Gothic after a visit to Scandinavia'. This was the style used by CH James for large public commissions like Norwich City Hall. Calkin's wood-block fabric design, 'Rope and Thistle', originally designed for 'Hornbeams', was printed on a commercial scale for use in the Marriage Suite and another of her designs was specially commissioned for the Lady Members' Room.

With her husband's career prospering and another war looming, Calkin's career entered another stage. Commissioned designs for print featured less in the order book to be replaced by more lengthy 'one-off' projects. 'Hornbeams' was requisitioned and the family evacuated to Chipping Camden with its sympathetic Arts and Crafts associations. For the Artists' General Benevolent Institute she made forays to John Lewis's war damage sale in order to run up

Garden front of No. 1 Hampstead Way, designed by CH James in 1923.

multiple small garments for bombed-out children; and now there was more time and opportunity for landscapes and flower paintings. The collection of floral illustrations and hand-written poems was well received when she exhibited them together in St George's Gallery, Cork Street, in 1957. A reviewer in *Art News and Review* urged publishers to consider 'the de luxe edition which it certainly deserves', but in the austerity of the post-war period publishers were unwilling to risk the expense of such a publication. Equally dispiriting were the requests from the Medici Society, who purchased two sheets of flower studies for posters in 1957: the colours had to be crudely 'bumped up' to allow for the technical limitations of colour reproduction and also for prevailing market tastes.

Undaunted, Calkin James focused on the two strands of work in which her creative freedom was unhampered by commercial or technological restraints: calligraphy and a renewed enthusiasm for printmaking, exhibiting prints regularly at the annual Royal Academy Summer Exhibitions. One melancholy

'Hornbeams', Winnington Road, Hampstead
Garden Suburb, designed by CH James, 1936.
Calkin James collaborated with her husband
in the design, furnishing and equipping of this
house. Before the completion of the building
she had a large printing table specially
constructed in the attic where she produced
many yards of block-printed curtaining.
Photograph by CH James.

The new City Hall, Norwich, 1938, designed
by CH James and SR Pierce.
Photograph reproduced with permission
from the *Architects Journal*.

Opposite: Rope and Thistle block-printed
textile, 1936, designed and printed by Calkin
James for 'Hornbeams'. Later this pattern was
printed commercially, in a different colourway
of silver greys, for use in the Marriage Suite
of the new Norwich City Hall.

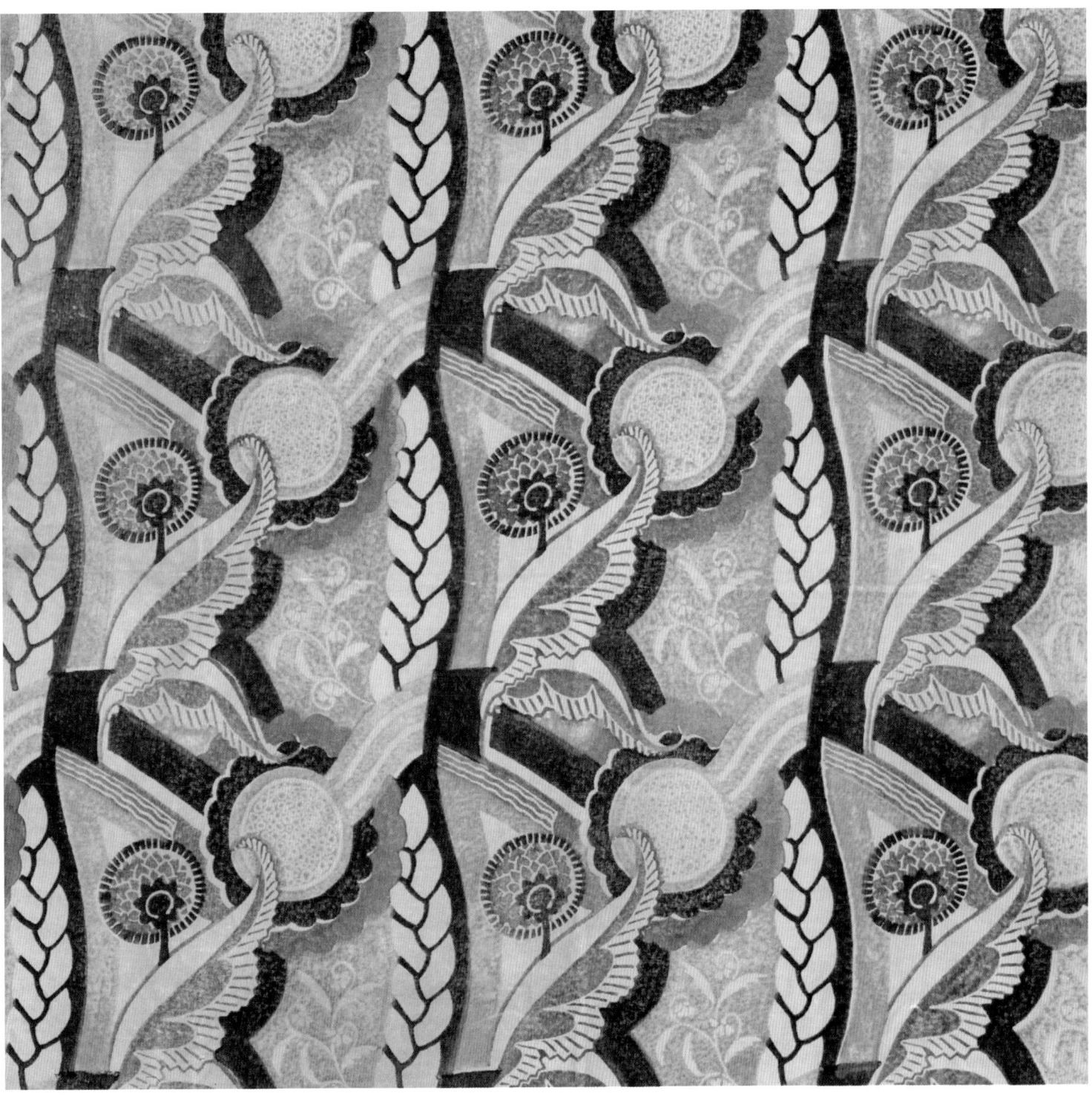

project was a book of names of the local war dead for St Peter's Church, Brighton, and another, prepared for the London Press Club, contained the names of journalists and news photographers of the Empire who had been killed in the War. A Roll of Honour is a sustained act of repetition, and Calkin James retained this discipline of continuity. Yet there is a lively feeling that each name is an individual rather than one of a monotonous list. Technically this is accomplished by the organisation of the separate pieces of information, by the style, weight and colour of the writing, and by simple ornaments variously designed to fit the spaces between names and ranks. Her belief that each of those names represented an undying idea of God would also influence her approach to such a task.

In 1949, the London County Council invited Margaret Calkin James to represent them on the Board of Directors of the Central School of Arts and Crafts. She declined, though pleased that her long-standing professional status was thus acknowledged. Ever since her days as a student at the Central she had lived by the belief that art – and life – had a serious moral purpose. Such a sense of direction to her life gave her great verve and confidence which was reflected in her designs and was the impetus behind her consistent pursuit of simplicity, usefulness and beauty.

'Fritillary' pattern block-printed textile, 1936, designed and hand-printed by Calkin James for 'Hornbeams'.

Margaret Calkin James photographed for the *Welwyn Times* in November 1981 to publicise an exhibition of her wool embroideries at the Central Library, Welwyn Garden City.
All the embroideries were created in the twelve years since a severe stroke in 1969 had deprived her of speech and the use of her right hand. However she taught herself to embroider using her left hand only. The exhibition was organised by her daughter, Elizabeth Argent as a contribution to the International Year of the Disabled.

Needlepoint sampler designed and worked by Calkin James using her left hand after she was disabled by a stroke in 1969.

Opposite: Hexagonal quilt pieced by hand from scraps, with *MCJ 1955* embroidered in one corner.

FELIX SCRIBO
SCRIPSI FELICIOR
Margaret Calkin James